Hostels Shopping

Checklist on Traveling Australia in Hostels

© Copyright 2018 Grizzly Publishing - All rights reserved.

This document is geared towards providing exact and reliable information in regards to the topic and issue covered. The publication is sold on the idea that the publisher is not required to render an accounting, officially permitted, or otherwise, qualified services. If advice is necessary, legal or professional, a practiced individual in the profession should be ordered.

From a Declaration of Principles which was accepted and approved equally by a Committee of the American Bar Association and a Committee of Publishers and Associations.

In no way is it legal to reproduce, duplicate, or transmit any part of this document by either electronic means or in printed format. Recording of this publication is strictly prohibited and any storage of this document is not allowed unless with written permission from the publisher. All rights reserved.

The information provided herein is stated to be truthful and consistent, in that any liability, in terms of inattention or otherwise, by any usage or abuse of any policies, processes, or directions contained within is the solitary and utter responsibility of the recipient reader. Under no circumstances will any legal responsibility or blame be held against the publisher for any reparation, damages, or monetary loss due to the information herein, either directly or indirectly.

Respective authors own all copyrights not held by the publisher.

The information herein is offered for informational purposes solely and is universal as so. The presentation of the information is without a contract or any type of guarantee assurance.

The trademarks that are used are without any consent, and the publication of the trademark is without permission or backing by the trademark owner. All trademarks and brands within this book are for clarifying purposes only and are the owned by the owners themselves, not affiliated with this document.

GRIZZLY PUBLISHING

www.grizzlypublishing.com

Introduction

Nineteen UNESCO World Heritage sites, such as the Tasmanian Wilderness, the Great Barrier Reef and the Sydney Opera House, in addition to the stunning natural scenery, make Australia one of the top destinations in the world to visit. The Outback, with its immense expanse of vivid reddish-brown earth, its lush jungles and its pristine beaches all call to tourists to come and enjoy them throughout the year. From outdoor activities such as snorkeling and surfing, to luxury shopping malls and quaint markets, cultural and artistic events and excellent cuisine, it is little wonder why millions of visitors flock to Australia each year.

Australia remains one of the best and most popular destinations for backpackers. As a result, there are countless hostels throughout the country, from top cities such as Perth, Melbourne and Sydney, as well as smaller cities such as Cairns, Tasmania, Adelaide and Brisbane, in addition to those scattered in quiet villages and rural areas.

Hostels are a great way of experiencing Australia no matter what the reason may be for your visit. Maybe you're coming over on a working holiday visa and need to save as much as you can on your expenses, or perhaps you are looking for a new travel experience? Whatever the reason why you are opting to stay in a hostel over a hotel, there are countless places for you to choose from, each one featuring their own unique characteristics and amenities.

Staying in a hostel instead of a hotel will not only find that they will save money (a lot of money in some destinations), but it gives you so much flexibility when it comes to your travel plans. Once you have decided on a destination, you can book a hostel for a few nights, and then move on to your next destination. And, for a bonus, you're more than likely to find someone who is planning to travel to your next destination as well – which means, if you like, you've just made a friend to accompany you if you want them to!

Australia is still regarded by many as a 'rite of passage,' and because of this, it frequently makes the top ten of backpacker destinations. Hostels have become a necessity for those looking for affordable, safe and convenient accommodation.

In the past, hostels have been regarded as dirty, and people have been daunted about staying in them but, in recent years, there has been a shift in attitudes. In reality, they can be fantastic places to stay at, providing you pick the right one for your needs.

It is essential that you choose the right type of hostel for your needs. For example, if you want somewhere quiet where you're not going to get woken up for the hundredth time because of blaring music from the bar next door, then don't choose a hostel connected to it. Hostels with bars or pubs attached to them are referred to as party hostels, and are best suited for guests who like to party a lot. This type of hostel has a strict policy regarding taking personal liquor into the accommodation simply because they prefer you to purchase it from the bar. However, if you are looking to sleep, then these are not the right hostels for you.

There are dozens of websites that cater specifically to hostels in Australia, as well as other hostel websites that feature other destinations throughout the world. Reviews are a great way of finding out if the hostel is the right one for you, and don't forget that most reviewers will comment on their own experiences at that particular hostel, rather than the hostel itself, which is always a good thing to keep in mind.

Many people who regularly stay in hostels will choose a place with a mid-range price, with free Wi-Fi, a kitchen and 24-hour reception. Since many hostels will have to pay a charge on the websites where they advertise though, it is sometimes cheaper to book directly through them, instead of through a middle-man. It is easy enough to contact the hostel direct, and if your plans change, then it is easy to cancel without incurring any fees.

You can stay in hostels throughout the year, but for those deciding to travel off-season, it is imperative that you contact the hostel in advance to make certain that they will still be open for business. In some places, especially rural or off the beaten track places, some hostels will close down during the non-peak times. During peak times, they can get full quite quickly. If you are the spontaneous type of traveler, you may discover that you have nowhere to sleep if you don't book in advance. Therefore, it is extremely important that you book accommodation in advance. Many places will refund some of your money if you decide to move onto a new destination before your original chosen date, or you can extend your stay if you wish to stay on longer.

TABLE OF CONTENTS

INTRODUCTION IV
CHAPTER ONE – WHAT IS A HOSTEL AND WHY SHOULD YOU CHOOSE ONE? 1
CHAPTER TWO - TIPS FOR STAYING IN A HOSTEL 3
CHAPTER THREE - WHO STAYS IN A HOSTEL? 6
CHAPTER FOUR - WHAT TYPES OF ROOMS DO HOSTELS HAVE? 7
CHAPTER FIVE – PROS AND CONS TO STAYING IN HOSTELS 9
CHAPTER SIX – HOW TO BOOK A HOSTEL 13
CHAPTER SEVEN – HOW HOSTELS CAN MAKE YOU A MORE CONFIDENT TRAVELLER 15
CHAPTER EIGHT – THE ONLY HOSTEL PACKING GUIDE YOU WILL EVER NEED 19
CHAPTER NINE – TIPS FOR MAKING NEW FRIENDS IN HOSTELS 22
CHAPTER TEN – EVERYTHING YOU NEED TO KNOW ABOUT STAYING IN A HOSTEL FOR THE FIRST TIME . 25
CHAPTER ELEVEN – THINGS YOU LEARN ABOUT YOURSELF WHEN STAYING IN A HOSTEL 28
CHAPTER TWELVE – HOW TO CHOOSE A GOOD HOSTEL 30
CONCLUSION 33

Chapter One

What Is a Hostel and Why Should You Choose One?

Hostels can be defined as low budget accommodation that several travelers will share at one time. Instead of booking a room per night, guests will book a bed per night. This bed that the guest books may be located within a room or dorm room with up to twenty other travelers, either male, female or mixed.

Bathrooms consist of dormitory style facilities, which generally feature a row of sinks and several shower stalls, with one or two bathrooms situated on a floor, unlike that of a hotel room which tends to boast an en-suite, private bathroom. There is much more interaction within hostels than hotels, but there is less personal service or privacy than a normal hotel.

However, there are some hostels which can offer private rooms with private bathrooms. Even with this, the prices charged by hostels are far less than you would pay at hotels or guesthouses since you share the space with other travelers. Even if you choose to stay in a private room, you can still get many other extras, including a communal kitchen, events, and free Internet, thus saving you money.

The price of a hostel will vary depending on a number of factors such as where you want to stay (cities such as Sydney and Melbourne will be much more expensive than Adelaide, for example), how many people you want to stay with (a room with twenty beds is cheaper than a room with four beds), and what date you plan on arriving. The best way of ensuring you keep the costs down and to make sure you get the hostel you want, is by booking as far in advance as you can, particularly in high season when accommodation gets sold out in a short time.

Hostels are also one of the safest places to stay in when traveling throughout the country. Because you are sharing your space with other people, there is always someone around you, and if you don't return back to the hostel after a night out, they can and will sound the alarm for you – something that would not happen if you were staying in a hotel.

In addition to this, most hostels will feature security around the clock, with 24-hour reception, and card keys so that only those guests staying in a hostel will have access to the hostel. Most hostels will have lockers within the dorm rooms for you to stow away your personal belongings when you go out or at night. As long as you take the same security measures as you would when staying at a hotel, a hostel can be just as safe.

Chapter Two

Tips for Staying in a Hostel

Staying in a hostel can be a bit daunting if you haven't stayed in one before, but you shouldn't fear the unknown! Read on to discover the best tips for staying in a hostel in Australia for the first time.

Read the Reviews

Prior to clicking on the Book Now button, you should always try and research as much as you can about a hostel. Reviews are there to help you make up your mind about a place. You will get two types of reviews – personal reviews and professional reviews. A personal review is provided by someone who has previously stayed at a hostel and will tell you what they liked or didn't like about their time there. Most personal reviews will be extremely positive or extremely negative. Professional reviews tend to give details on the facilities and amenities provided by the hostel, and give a more balanced point of view compared to personal reviews.

Book the Right Hostel and the Right Type of Room

It is important that you book the right hostel and type of room for your needs. Some hostels offer mixed rooms, and some will offer same-sex rooms. If you are a woman and would prefer to stay in a room with other women, then a hostel that only offers coed rooms will not be the right choice for you. If you don't want to be in a room with twenty people, try and choose a hostel that offers small sized rooms. A comfortable stay is a happy stay, especially if you are a solo traveler.

Book One Night

It is a good idea to only book one night at a hostel for your first stay in case you find that you don't like it or if you have a terrible time. That way, you can book a different hostel and not feel obligated to stay, or if you did like it, then you can extend your stay.

Bring Your Personal Toiletries

Do not expect the toiletries that you would normally find in a hotel to be within your hostel. In addition, most hostels do not provide towels, so you will need to bring your own along with shampoo, conditioner, toothpaste, soap etc. Some hostels do not provide sheets, so it is important that you look at what the amenities the hostel offers before you click on the Book Now button.

Flip Flops are Your Friend

One of the top things you will need to bring is a good pair of flip flops. In addition to being comfortable footwear while out and about, they are essential for when you hit the shower. The shower stalls are used by countless people from all over the globe, so they are a precautionary measure against fungi and bacteria.

Be Thoughtful and Considerate

For however long you plan to stay, you should treat your new roommates as you would like to be treated yourself. If you wish to be treated considerately and thoughtfully, you should treat others the same way. If you arrive in the room late in the evening, or have to leave early in the mornings, then try and be as quiet as you can. It's always best to have your things ready and prepared the night before so you're not disturbing the others.

Take Care of Your Valuables

You need to keep your passport and your money and other valuables safe at all times. Ideally, you should keep these on your person or in a locker. If your hostel doesn't come equipped with lockers, see if your things can be kept safe at the reception. The people you are sharing your room with may seem nice, but it's best to be safe rather than sorry.

If You're Unhappy, Talk to the Manager

Managers are there to help you whenever things go wrong. If something is wrong, or you're not having a good experience, talk to the manager and see if there is something they can do to rectify the situation. Some things they may say no to, but they are there to ensure everything runs smoothly.

Chapter Three

Who Stays in a Hostel?

One of the top reasons why so many people will opt to stay in a hostel over a hotel is the fact that you get to meet new people from all over the world. You just don't know who you are going to meet when you open your room, adding an element of surprise and excitement that you just don't get if you're traveling solo and staying in a private hotel room.

While most people think that staying in hostels is for twenty-somethings on a gap year, the truth is that people of all ages and backgrounds will choose a hostel. It's not uncommon to see a couple in their sixties touring from a European country stay at a hostel with a young family, a professional in their thirties, or even artists of all kinds. Every day is a surprise as to who you will meet. That's what makes staying at a hostel so unique and thrilling, and why so many people continue to do it.

Hostels are for everybody. No matter how old you are, where you come from, what you want to do – everyone can stay at a hostel. Most of the people who stay in hostels do so because they are on a budget and are solo travelers, mostly under the age of 40. But since many hostels are upgrading and becoming more stylish and offering luxuries, they have become popular with many others who don't have to worry about a budget.

Chapter Four

What Types of Rooms Do Hostels Have?

If you are opting to stay in a hostel for your next trip to Australia, you will need to choose a room that suits your requirements. Therefore, read on to discover what types of rooms to expect in a hostel.

Dorms

Most people will expect to stay in a dorm style room, which are, essentially, big rooms that can sleep typically between four and twenty people at a time. Beds are usually bunk beds in order to accommodate more people. Those who opt to stay in a dorm room will pay a fraction of the price of a private hotel room. Generally speaking, the price is cheaper if you choose to stay in a room with more people.

These dorm rooms will come in varying sizes and shapes. You can find cheap rooms with basic facilities, to the more luxurious types with double mattresses and better amenities. Whatever type of bed you book, most dorm style beds will tend to include a privacy curtain, a power socket so you can charge your phone or laptop, and a reading light. Some will include an en-suite bathroom to be shared with the others in your room instead of everyone on the same floor as you.

Some dorm rooms will have female or male only rooms. When you go to book your room, it should be listed on the room types option.

Private Rooms

Private rooms are an option for travelers who want privacy but at a cheaper rate than a standard hotel room and still enjoy all the fun a hostel brings. Many hostels offer private rooms, generally for couples, older guests, or for families. They do cost more than the standard dorm rooms, but are still cheaper than hotels. However, most private rooms do come with an en-suite bathroom, along with all the other facilities guests can enjoy, such as events, social areas and communal kitchens.

The price of a private room will largely vary depending on the hostel and its location. Some cities in Australia are more expensive than others, and beachfront accommodation will certainly be more expensive than others in quieter locations.

Chapter Five

Pros and Cons to Staying in Hostels

If you haven't stayed at a hostel before, it can be a bit daunting to think about booking one for the first time. Read on to discover the pros and cons to staying in hostels when visiting Australia.

Advantages to Staying at a Hostel

They Are Inexpensive

Let's face it, traveling can be an expensive experience, no matter how long or hard we save up for it. Hotels will certainly take a large chunk out of your budget, but hostels are generally a fraction of the price. As mentioned before, the price of a hostel will depend on when you arrive, which city you stay in, where it is located, and what type of room you opt for. However, the price is generally much lower than a standard hotel room.

You Can Travel in Groups

If you are travelling with a group of people, finding accommodation to fit everyone within your budget can be a little tricky. Some dorm rooms can accommodate up to twenty people at any one time – this means you can all stay together and stops any unnecessary arguments about who is sharing with whom.

They Can Be Found in Most Places

Australia is a large country, and even cities and towns can be massive compared to home. Hostels can be found in all large Australian cities, in most towns, and even in the most rural of destinations, making them ideal for those who want to see everything the country has to offer.

Most Hostels Feature Kitchens

Eating out every day can be expensive, and sometimes you just want to cook something for yourself. Most hostels come with a full equipped kitchen with a fridge, so you can use the facilities whenever you need to.

Some Include Breakfast

Some hostels will include breakfast in the price of your stay. Usually, this tends to include toast, cereal and fruit, although this will vary from hostel to hostel, and you should check the amenities offered.

Fun Group Activities

Hostels like to have happy guests and so will keep them happy by offering fun activities. Some of these events can include a happy hour at the attached bar/pub, games in the common room, or even a workshop.

You Get to Meet so Many Different People

Hostels are not just for people who have recently finished or waiting to go to college/university; many different people have begun using hostels. From lawyers to politicians, from artists to couples on a romantic trip, from elderly people to young families, you get to meet so many people from all over the world, just wanting to explore Australia.

They Offer Security

Sometimes people are a little scared to choose a hostel because of fears of personal security. The majority of hostels will have a strict policy regarding who comes into their establishment. If you are worried about your valuables, most hostels offer lockers and safes to keep them secure.

They are Unique

Many hotels tend to blur from one to the next, but with hostels you are guaranteed a once in a lifetime experience. Every hostel is unique, and that's just one of the reasons why they are so popular.

Disadvantages to Staying at a Hostel

Lack of Privacy

If you are choosing to stay at a hostel, then don't expect much privacy. You will be sharing a room with multiple people whom you've never met before and some may not understand the concept of privacy. Some beds will have a privacy curtain, but others may not. Some hostels may offer double or private rooms, but these tend to be booked quick and may not be available when you require a room.

Dorm Style Bathrooms

The bathrooms in hostels are generally dorm-style, meaning there are several shower stalls in one bathroom. Typically, you can expect one bathroom per floor.

Limited Staff

Most hotels have staff available 24 hours a day, but this may not be the case when it comes to hostels. This means that if you somehow forget or lose the key to your room when you're out one night, you may risk not being able to get in until a member of staff comes in.

Curfews

Some hostels have a curfew, unlike that of hotels. This means that if you are not in the hostel before a particular time, you can't get in until the next morning.

There is a Risk of Having Your Belongings Stolen

There is an element of risk with having items taken when it comes to sharing a room with many people or even with members of staff. If there isn't a locker or a personal safe, this risk increases.

Strangers

Unless you book a private room, you will be sharing a room with up to twenty people. Sharing a room with so many people can be a little frightening to those who have never stayed in a hostel before.

Locations

The location of many hostels in metro areas can be situated near abandoned or unused buildings. These locations can be extremely convenient, although they may seem a little sketchy in the evenings at first.

Older Buildings

A large number of hostels are situated within older buildings. As a result, you may find there is no elevator, or one that breaks down often, the plumbing may be old, the heating may not work efficiently, or the air conditioning may not work at all.

Chapter Six

How to Book a Hostel

If you have chosen to stay at a hostel for part or all of your trip to Australia, then you have made a fantastic and exciting decision. The first thing you need to do is to decide which cities you are visiting and on what dates.

Next, head to one of the many hostel booking websites. Type in the city of your choice and the date when you are arriving. On many booking sites, you will see a dropdown box or a box where you can tick for features that are important. These include how many guests are travelling, a rating system, what currency you wish it to be displayed in (such as US dollars, UK sterling, Euros, Australian dollars etc.), room types (single private, double private, mixed dorm, male dorm, female dorm etc.), features, location, and payment types.

Once you have ticked all the features that you require, you will see a number of accommodations that match your requirements. You should go through all of them, seeing which one you find yourself drawn to. It is important that you read through all the reviews, especially the negative ones, to ensure that you are going to be comfortable there.

After you are satisfied with the selection of your hostel, all you need to do is click the Book Now button. Ensure that your dates are correct, as is the type of room you require and how many guests. Some hostels only require a percentage to book the room in advance, and all you do is pay the remaining balance on arrival. Please note, some hostels require cash payments or card payments only – it is best to double check this before paying.

Another thing to look at is the hostel's refund and cancellation policies. Some hostels will charge the full amount of the stay booked if you do not cancel within a certain timeframe. Again, it is best to double check these policies before paying anything.

Once satisfied with everything, all you have to do is simply fill out your details (name, address, contact details, email address, etc.), and your payment details. Once you've ticked the box that says, "*I accept the terms and conditions*," just click on the Pay Now button and that's it! You will receive a confirmation in your email box which should print out a copy for when you travel.

Chapter Seven

How Hostels Can Make You a More Confident Traveller

If you have never travelled on your own before, a solo trip may make you feel nervous. Even if you are travelling with someone else, you may feel scared. However, hostels can make you feel more confident while traveling.

The hostel in which you stay at will be your home for however long you're staying for. Your roommates quickly become friends and when you are with friends, you become comfortable and more confident. Respect and friendship can help you come out of your shell and you soon become secure in your travels.

You Meet People from Different Countries

The first question you are most likely to hear from another person in the same hostel as you is typically *"Where are you from?"* You may not even know their names until the following day, but you'll know where each of your room-mates is from. After a few minutes chatting and getting to know each other, it isn't unusual to find that you've already made plans to go down to the beach with your new friend from Spain or Japan. If you are worried that you may not know what to say to other people, all you have to do is smile, say hello, and introduce yourself. The rest just flows and it's normal for hostels. Be yourself and see what happens.

Because Australia is one of the top tourist destinations in the world, millions of people from all over the globe make their way here. Where else would you meet someone from Sweden, France, China, Brazil, Egypt, the UK, and India all in one place? Nowhere but a hostel!

You Get Used to Being Uneasy

The first time you stay at a hostel will be the most uncomfortable, but this is natural. You're in a foreign country staying in a room with twenty people you have not met until that day. It some respects, it can be a little intimidating, but you should remember that this is a good thing! It helps you to open up, learn how to communicate with people through more than just language, learn new habits and customs you may not have come into contact with, and it forces you to step outside your comfort zone. People tend to thrive when faced with new challenges, leaving you with more confidence in the long run.

You Become a Community

Just because you are sharing a room with other people, doesn't mean that you have to make friends with everyone. However, they soon become your community, and you their community. The respect and kindness they give to you, you should give back to them. Everyone takes responsibility within their community. This means being quiet during the early hours of the morning and clearing up any messes you make in the bathroom or kitchen.

Hostel stays give you the opportunity to create new friendships and experiences with other people in the same situation as you. Talking to others in the same hostel as you give you this opportunity – the opportunity to become a community, something you just can't experience in a hotel, even if you are only staying 24 hours.

You Learn Something New Every Time

Staying in a hostel in Australia gives you the chance to learn something new every time you visit. Have you ever wanted to learn surfing or snorkeling? Have you ever fancied yourself a singer but don't know where to start? (Karaoke night in the hostel can certainly help you build your confidence in this). Most hostels offer events and experiences for guests to try, from making local dishes, to cultural excursions, to sporting activities nearby.

When you're at home, it is easy to fall back into your normal routine (eat, sleep, go to work, deal with kids, etc.), but when you stay at a hostel, you have the freedom to do anything you want! And since the others staying with you are typically in the same boat as you, they will be the first ones to cheer you on, because they want you to cheer them on, too! The activities offered will depend on the hostel, its location, and where in the country you are, but even if they don't offer what you fancy, they are in the position to help you find out. Hostels, therefore, are one of the best ways to experience Australia, as well as yourself.

You Learn to Be Who You Truly Are

It's very easy to hide who you are in the real world. College and work life can force you to be someone you don't really want to be (for example, you may have to be more serious and professional). However, when you stay at a hostel, you can let it all go and be yourself. The people staying in the hostel with you are more open-minded than anyone else you are likely to meet. And because of that, you can have the confidence to drop that serious mask and just be yourself.

No one is judging you when you stay at a hostel. They are far more interested in having a good time than analyzing you. Yes, they will be interested in learning who you are and where you're from, and whether you have any tips or advice, but on the whole, they are more interested in having fun. This gives you the opportunity to be who you are, and learn more about what you like to do.

You Learn More about the World

Let's face it, the media can paint the world as a terrible place. Sometimes, it can enhance our fears of what's out there waiting, and can put us off traveling. People from different countries – people who you don't know – may have you feeling nervous. However, when you stay at a hostel, you quickly learn that everyone shares a love of traveling and new experiences and are, in fact, just like you. You meet every type of person at a hostel – people with different skin colors, different nationalities, different social classes, different religions, etc. None of it matters when you stay at a hostel – everyone puts on a genuine positive atmosphere because it makes the trip so much better (however, you may meet a few negative people, but you will come into contact with these types of people no matter where you go, even at home).

When you stay at a hostel, you learn more about the world. Not only do you learn about the country and way of life in the country that you're visiting, but you learn more about the customs and habits of strangers from all over the world. You learn more about the world this way than you would in a classroom. Everyone is out of their comfort zones and they're embracing strangers from all over the world, uniting over your love of travel. And when you go back home, you take that experience, and that unique feeling, with you.

Chapter Eight

The Only Hostel Packing Guide You Will Ever Need

There are numerous reasons why hostels are a great option when traveling to Australia. One of the best reasons is that they are less expensive than hotels. However, they do feature less amenities than hotels, so it is important to pay attention to what you are packing. Read on to discover the top things you need to pack when staying at a hostel.

Toiletries

Many hotels will offer complimentary shampoos, soaps and razors. However, when you are staying at a hostel, you won't get these. Therefore, you should pack your own shampoos, soaps, conditioners, all of which you can find in travel sizes at your local supermarkets. Other things to bring includes sunscreen, deodorants, hairbrushes and insect repellent.

Flip Flops

A pair of flip flops will be your best friend. Known as thongs in Australia, you will need them when heading into the communal showers. You don't want to pick up foot fungi as a souvenir of your time Down Under. You will need a separate pair for the showers if you use them as normal footwear.

Towels

Some hostels do not provide towels, and may charge you to use them. Remember to bring a light towel that dries quickly, not just for the showers, but also for the beach (if it's a beach destination).

Something to Entertain You

It doesn't matter how busy your itinerary is, there will always be times when you can just relax and not do anything. A Kindle, iPad, or even a deck of cards will help entertain you when you have some quiet time. And if you bring a book, many times you can swap it with someone else once you've finished reading it.

A Good Quality Padlock

There will be times when you need to store your luggage at an airport, a train station, or at the hostel. A good quality lock on your bag can help secure your personal belongings, as well as stopping you from being charged for one by the hostel.

Sleeping Aids

When you stay in a hostel, you will most likely come across someone who snores. Some people may come in late after partying all night, and others may need to leave early in the morning. In this case, it is best if you bring earplugs and a sleep mask to help you get some sleep.

An Adapter

Before you set off, make sure you have purchased and packed an adapter. A universal adapter is preferred if you want to travel to another part of the world afterwards. An adapter helps you to charge your phone, Kindle, iPad, etc., so you can contact people back home.

Just as there are things you do need to pack, there are some things which you DON'T need to pack. These items take up unnecessary room in your pack and will weigh you down.

Sleeping Bag

Many first-timers think they will need a sleeping bag, but you don't! Most hostels will provide the bed linen, so unless you are planning to camp out, you don't need to bring a sleeping bag.

Hair Straighteners or Dryers

These types of gadgets are just not necessary. They are big, heavy and bulky, and will take up a lot of room in your bag. Many of the nicer hostels will provide hair dryers.

Expensive Items

Do not bring expensive items such as fancy (or sentimental) jewelry, or fancy laptops or professional cameras (unless you are a professional photographer). A camera is a must item for most travelers, but unless you absolutely need it, leave the rest of your items at home so you don't spend all your time worrying about them.

How to Pack

Get the Right Backpack

Most people who stay in a hostel chose to travel light and with a backpack instead of traditional suitcases as lockers tend not to be that big. It is a good idea to purchase a backpack that opens at the front instead of at the top, like many hiking backpacks. This allows you to get to all your belongings without having to take everything out first.

Common Sense

When you pack your bags before setting off, remember to use some common sense when it comes to safety. Most people will not touch your stuff, but it is always best to be safe rather than sorry. Keep all your items in a padlocked compartment within your backpack, separated from each other. Pay particular attention to where you store your money, phones and passport.

Chapter Nine

Tips for Making New Friends in Hostels

One of the best experiences you could ever have is traveling by yourself and staying in a hostel. There is so much freedom in staying in a hostel by yourself; you don't have to compromise with anyone else over where you're going, or what you want to do – you decide it all. You can set your own pace instead of someone else's. However, even those who have travelled solo several times can get a sense of melancholy or even feel lonely. One of the best aspects of staying in a hostel is that you are always surrounded, and it is easy enough to make new friends with whom you can share adventures during your stay. Read on to discover some of the best tips for making new friends in hostels.

Don't be Shy!

Easier said than done, of course, if you are naturally shy and question if you are, indeed, able to make new friends while staying in a new place with strangers. First, take a deep breath and try not to worry. Try to leave your shyness at home and be prepared to talk to new people. What's the worst thing that can happen? You've already travelled by yourself and stepped out of your comfort zone, so what's talking to someone? Many travelers are shy, and many aren't. The beauty of staying in a hostel is that you get to meet both types of people. Naturally friendly people tend to go out of their way and talk to people, so if they talk to you first, smile, say hi, and try your best to let the shyness disappear.

Be Flexible

You will meet so many people from all around the world, each with their own unique characters and personalities. Some you will only speak to while in your room, some you might share a drink with at the end of the day, and others you may actually become traveling companions for a time. Each one will make an impact on you, just as you will on them. Try to be flexible, and open up to different cultures and appreciate their own individual personalities.

Share a Dorm Instead of a Private Room

Many hostels will offer private single or double rooms, but when you share a dorm room with other people, it gives you a push to talk to others. Maybe you need to charge your phone, but you've lost your adapter? Ask someone in the room if you could borrow one from them until you can buy a new one. It would be much harder to make a friend if you're stuck by yourself in a private room.

Engage in Some of the Activities Offered by the Hostel

Hostels are a great way of meeting new people, and the staff know this better than anyone! This is why most hostels offer a variety of activities for their guests. It can be anything from learning how to make a regional dish, from sports, karaoke, an excursion, surfing – the list is endless! Also, when you are not out sight-seeing, try and spend as much time in the hostel communal areas because it isn't unusual for some of the greatest traveling adventures to start from a simple conversation between two people.

Walking Tours

Many hostels will offer free walking tours around the local neighborhood. Many Australian cities also offer walking tours; when you go on one of these, not only do you get to learn about the local city and its culture and heritage, but you get to talk with other people who are interested. Wonderful friendships have started with nothing but a few simple words exchanged with someone on the same tour as you.

Drinking Times!

Some hostels are attached to a bar or pub, and some will offer a pub crawl. This is where a group of people will visit several bars over the night and enjoy themselves with a few (or several) drinks. It's not uncommon for one person in the same hostel as you to invite you all out for a drink. This is a great way to socialize; a drink can help relax and ease your shyness, and make new friends. In addition, the more people you're with, the safer you are. The staff at the hostel can always recommend the best places to go.

Talk to Someone Who's Not from Your Country

Many people from all over the world will opt to stay in a hostel for various reasons. If you want to make new friends, why not start a conversation with someone from a different culture. Many people can speak English to varying degrees, and they may be appreciative of a friendly face if they are feeling lonely.

Use Technology

If you're in town for a few nights and want to meet up with someone new, use technology. You can easily download various dating and friend apps, so you can meet someone you would never normally meet back home. You don't have to date someone on these apps – sometimes you can just make new friends with them.

Chapter Ten

Everything You Need to Know About Staying in a Hostel for the First Time

Okay, you've scoured the websites, fallen in love with a hostel that fits your requirements, and clicked on Pay Now. You have just booked yourself an amazing time. Staying in a hostel means an exciting experience, whether you have travelled extensively in the past, or if this is your first time. If this is your first time, you may be a little anxious about what to expect and what the common rules are.

There is no 'set' guidelines for guests who stay at hostels, but there are some general things that you pick up along the way. However, read on to discover everything you need to know about staying in a hostel for the first time.

Making Friends

You may think that you're there for only two nights and that girl who is reading your favorite author doesn't want to be interrupted. However, don't assume she doesn't want to be interrupted. Go over and say hello. Introduce yourself and if you want to get to know her more, suggest a drink (in the communal area, of course), or lunch and get to know her and what she has experienced so far. You will meet so many interesting people by staying in hostels. Some people may be traveling for the first time, others may be on a three-year tour of the world. You may have more in common with them than you initially think. And it all starts by saying "hello."

Coming in Late ... or Early

Being away from home means you can let your hair down and cut loose. Staying up drinking all night with new friends sounds like a great idea – and to a certain degree, it is. However, if you're stumbling into the dorm room at three am drunk, waking other people up, it's a sure-fire way to make people hate you and ruin their experience. Do not get so drunk that you are being sick all over the place. No one, including you, will thank you for it.

Curfews

You may think it is easy to stay up all night without disturbing anyone or going out drinking all night. However, if you think by using headphones and whispering to friends on WeChat or Skype that you're not disturbing anyone, think again. Like being sick on the floor from drinking too much, whispering on the phone at two am is another way of getting on other people's nerves. Most hostels have a curfew, and most will have lights off by midnight. If you can't sleep after this time but still need something to do, try reading with a book light (with curtains drawn) or going to a communal area where you won't disturb anyone.

Getting Up Early

Your flight is at five am, so you need to be up early. You set the alarm on your phone, hit the snooze button a few times, and then when you eventually get out of bed, spend the next twenty minutes noisily rummaging around your bags. Even if you think you're being quiet, you're not. Be considerate of the fact that no one wants to be woken up at 3 am just because you have a flight. Ensure that all your belongings are packed the night before, use book lights instead of turning on the main light, try not to make too much sound, and don't hit the snooze button – get up the first time. Treat others the way you would wish to be treated yourself.

Flip Flops and the Showers

You may not need to wear flip flops or thongs in the shower at home, but in a hostel, you will always want a pair of them to shower with. If you don't, not only will you get disgusted looks from other guests, but you are more likely to bring home foot fungi with you as a reminder of your lack of common sense.

Kitchens

Most hostels have an equipped kitchen for guests to use. This is great because if you want to save some cash, you can cook at the hostel. However, unlike at your parents' house or a hotel, there is no one to clear up after you. You are responsible for cleaning up any mess you make. Not only do you need to clean every pot, pan, utensil, and clear up any spills, but you are required to dry it and put it away. Plus, you need to do a decent job. You will quickly become enemy number one if you do a poor, or no job at all.

Respecting Other People's Belongings

It's eleven pm and you're hungry. You can't be bothered to go out and get something and those cakes in the fridge are making your mouth water. The reality is that you cannot take someone else's food or anything else that doesn't belong to you. Respect other people's things, whether it's their food, drinks, clothes, or books.

Snoring

If you are a snorer, you can't help it. People understand that it can't be helped, but if you do snore, let your new roommates know in advance. If they are given a warning, they will appreciate it.

Chapter Eleven

Things You Learn About Yourself When Staying in a Hostel

When you stay at a hostel, you learn so many new things about yourself as well as new habits that you take back home with you. Some of the many things hostel travelers have learnt include:

You Learn How to Set a Budget, and Stick to It

Most people opt to stay in a hostel because it is a cheaper way of traveling. Even a three-star hotel can cost several hundred dollars for room only, but a hostel is just a fraction of the cost. When you stay in hostels, you learn how to set a budget and stick to it. Sometimes, instead of going out for dinner and drinks, you can spend a night in with new friends, cook a range of dishes, and share a few bottles of wine with each other. A cheap but cheerful night!

You Learn How to Take Care of Yourself

Let's face it, the normal nine to five grind can wear you down and sometimes you just need to get away to unwind. Hotels can be an expensive way of unwinding and can put more stress on you, but staying at a hostel allows you to unwind at a fraction of the cost. You can also find it exhausting doing all the sightseeing spots; sometimes all you need is to sit down and relax with a book.

You Learn How to Sleep Through Everything

Even if you're not a particularly heavy sleeper, once you've stayed in a hostel you find you can sleep through just about everything. Sometimes the smoke detector can set off the fire alarm, sending sirens blazing through the night, and sometimes the snoring of a fellow guest can wake you up several times in just one night. After a few nights, you soon find yourself being woken up less and less.

You Don't Need to Spend 30 Minutes in the Shower

Lazy mornings standing underneath the shower, the water cascading down your back ... ah, wonderful times. Even if you don't normally set a time limit on yourself when in the shower, when you stay a hostel, you soon learn that you don't need to spend thirty minutes in the shower to get every part clean. By the end of the first week, you'll soon discover you're washed and clean in five to ten minutes.

You're More Sociable than You May Think

Even the shyest of people may discover they're more social than they perceive themselves to be. When you're sharing a room with up to twenty people (some dorms can feature up to fifty guests), you won't find a lot of quiet or "me" time. Sharing a dorm means you've always got someone around you. It forces you to converse with others, be friendly, and make several new friends. You run into so many new, amazing people when you stay at a hostel, and you soon discover that you love it!

You're More Independent than What You Imagine

In addition to finding yourself more sociable than you think, you'll also discover you're more independent than you imagine. Many people like to stay in hostels because it gives them the chance to make new friends, as well as to save money, and to make your own travel arrangements, instead of relying on a travel agent or someone else.

Chapter Twelve

How to Choose a Good Hostel

When you are searching for a good hostel, you have your work cut out for you. There are a lot of depressing stories about hostels, but it comes down more to the people you are sharing with than the actual hostel itself. Nevertheless, it is important to do your research. You are searching for a hostel that knows what its guests want. Read on to discover how to choose a good hostel.

Don't Always Go for the Cheapest Option

Cheap is not always the best choice. When you are on a budget, it isn't surprising to go for the cheapest option you can find. However, do you really want to stay in a place with uncomfortable beds, unclean linen, and dirty showers just to save a few dollars?

Breakfast

A good way of stretching your budget is to find a hostel that serves breakfast. Not all hostels do serve it; look through the reviews and see what previous guests have said about the most important meal of the day. Some hostels only serve toast, tea, and coffee, while others offer more variety. By eating as much breakfast as you can at the hostel, you can cut down on your food budget.

Late Checkouts

Getting enough sleep is important to any traveler, so when booking a hostel, try to book one that has a checkout later than 10am. Some will offer noon day checkouts. Many hostels understand that sleep is important, especially to backpackers, and are more accommodating to this.

Free Lockers

Lockers are important to ensure that you don't have your belongings stolen. However, there are a few hostels out there that will charge extra to hire a locker, or have no lockers at all. You should never have to be charged to ensure your security. Lockers should always come free and as standard.

Free WIFI

While you don't always have to have Internet at a hostel, a hostel with free WIFI and a computer room will certainly make it much easier for you to communicate with friends and family back home. Particularly if there is a change in your travel schedule.

A Bar/Pub

While you don't necessarily have to have a bar at a hostel, and there are plenty of great hostels without them, having one gives you an easier time to socialize. Many hostels that feature a pub or bar offer happy hours and other activities to ensure that their guests have a great time interacting with each other and having fun. Plus, the drinks are generally much cheaper than other places.

A Communal Area

If your hostel doesn't have a bar, make sure it has a communal area which gives guests the chance to hang out and get to know one another. These communal areas are great for solo travelers who want to meet new people and have fun.

Offers Activities

Fantastic hostels offer a range of activities or excursions for their guests, such as pub crawls, walking tours, BBQs, cooking classes etc., so that guests can interact with each other and have a great time trying something new.

Well-informed Staff

One thing that you will certainly need to look out for in the reviews about your hostel is anything to do with staff. The staff at the hostel will either make or break your experience there. The majority of the staff are there to help you settle in, and be your first point of contact if you need anything, from disputes to information about the local area. If you are looking for a reliable place to rent a bike, or a great bar, then they are usually the ones who can point you in the right direction.

Conclusion

In many people's eyes, hostels have always been regarded as somewhere cheap for students on their gap year, traveling around before embarking on their studies or before starting their professional careers. In the past, hostels have been painted a grim picture – run down places in sketchy neighborhoods, with guests who like to party all night and sleep all day.

In reality, however, this is nothing like the truth. Hostels are one of the most amazing experiences any traveler could enjoy. In recent years, many hostels have become luxurious places to stay at, with a wide range of amenities and facilities, and artistic décor to really stand out in the crowd.

Hostels offer a wide range of experiences for all to discover. They allow you to meet people from all over the world, learning new customs, traditions and habits and forming friendships that can last from just a single day to many years. Some travelers have even found true love while staying at a hostel. The possibilities are endless.

When searching for a hostel, do not pick the first thing you see, or even the cheapest. Look around and find one that speaks to your requirements, and read through all the reviews to ensure it is going to be the best option for you.

Other Books by Grizzly Publishing

3 Book Australian Travel Bundle: How To Pack Your Bag When Traveling to Australia, Hostels Shopping: Checklist On Traveling Australia In Hostels & Flight Hacking: Learn The Secrets To Flying For Free

https://www.amazon.com/dp/B07C8FH4X9

How to Pack Your Bag When Traveling to Australia: Backpackers Essential Item List

https://www.amazon.com/dp/B077NY71TM

How To Teach English Overseas: Use Your Native Language To Fund Your Travels All Over The World

https://www.amazon.com/dp/B078K9FNGY

How to Build a Body That Attracts Beautiful Women: Forge a Masculine Body That Women Can't Resist

https://www.amazon.com/dp/B077PDGKJQ

Beijing In 72 Hours: Maximize Your Layover With Our 3 Day Plan

https://www.amazon.com/dp/B078XDBSRC

Printed in Great Britain
by Amazon